Merry
KITSCHMAS

Merry
KITSCHMAS

THE *Ultimate* HOLIDAY HANDBOOK

 by Michael D. Conway

photographs by PETER MEDILEK

CHRONICLE BOOKS

SAN FRANCISCO

Text copyright © 2004 by Michael D. Conway
Photographs copyright © 2004 by Peter Medilek
All rights reserved. No part of this book may be reproduced
in any form without written permission from the publisher.
Library of Congress Cataloging-in-Publication Data available.
ISBN: 0-8118-4211-8
Manufactured in Hong Kong
Photography by Peter Medilek/ClausNY, Inc.
Styling by Sonja Jurgens
Food Styling by Patrik Jaros/Food Look
Food Styling by Cyrille Allanic (Yellow Snow Cone)
Set Design by Rick Tesoro
Design by Azi Rad
Distributed in Canada by Raincoast Books
9050 Shaughnessy Street
Vancouver, British Columbia V6P 6E5
10 9 8 7 6 5 4 3 2 1
Chronicle Books LLC
85 Second Street
San Francisco, California 94105
www.chroniclebooks.com

The photographer wishes to thank Sonja Jurgens for her great talent and energy, Patrik Jaros for preparation of all the delicious feasts. Sarah and Ben Segal for opening up their stylish home. Stacey and Jonathan Levine for letting us play the grand piano, Regis Pean for the beautiful location and Brazilian sounds tracks, Rick Tesoro for his great ideas, Nancy Koltes and the MoMa Design Store for their gorgeous props.

Airstream is a registered trademark of Airstream, Inc. Aleene's Tacky Glue is a registered trademark of Aleene's Licensing Company, LLC. Bailey's Irish Cream is a registered trademark of R&A Bailey & Company, Ltd. Cointreau liqueur is a registered trademark of Cointreau Corporation. Godiva chocolate is a registered trademark of Godiva Brands, Inc. Goldschlager liqueur is a registered trademark of IDV North America, Inc. Grand Marnier is a registered trademark of Societe des Produits Marnier–Lapostolle. Jell-O is a registered trademark of General Foods Corporation. Plexiglass is a registered trademark of Rohm & Hans Company. Rit dye is a registered trademark of Conopco, Inc. Rose's lime juice is a registered trademark of L. Rose & Company, Ltd. Sculpey is a registered trademark of Polyform Products, Inc. Sprite is a registered trademark of The Coca-Cola Company. Tinkertoys are a registered trademark of Hasbro, Inc. Velcro is a registered trademark of Velcro Industries B.V. Worcestershire sauce is a registered trademark of Lea & Perrins, Inc. X-Acto is a registered trademark of X-Acto Crescent Products, Inc.

page 2: Kitschmas Tree Hive (page 117)
page 11: Junk for Joy Donut Tree (page 53)

Acknowledgments

This book is a salute to the queen of Kitschmas, Marilyn Conway, and her obsessive dedication to creating the sparkling Christmases of my childhood. Thanks to my father for suiting up as Santa in the middle of the night and creating a legendary close encounter that left a lifelong belief in the magic of Christmas.

I am eternally grateful to the following people who wrote this book alongside me: Ron Malott, for putting up with all the Kitschmas crap that littered our home for the past year. Katy Conway-Malott, for being my dream girl and not taking the dolls that Dad needed for his book. Kyle Conway-Malott, for being so joyfully funny and not eating ALL the ornaments on the White-Trash Tree. Theresa Langberg (my North Pole Test Kitchen), for searching out suet, cooking it, and actually tasting it. Jacquelyn Foreman, for her libation literacy and a loopy liquid lunch, full of Kitschmas spirits. Genine Smith, my muse, for listening and laughing. Gladys Huang and Atlas Design, LLC, for ten years of Christmas card fun. Joel Childress, for the Wreath of Franklins idea. Melinda McGraw, for her encouragement and inspiration. And Debra Lande, for the fabulous introduction to the folks at Chronicle.

Finally, I would like to acknowledge the Kitschmas elves that hammered away in their little workshops to make this book: editor, Mikyla Bruder, editorial assistant Leslie Davisson, designer Azi Rad, and photographer Peter Medilek. Their dedication and talent made this book sparkle like a dime-store Kitschmas tree.

chapter two

Deck the Halls
(and Walls and Doors and Floors)
with Lotsa Tchotchkes!
Fa, la, la, la, la, la, la, la, la

A few thoughts on Kitschmas

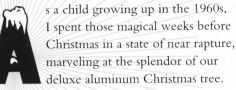

As a child growing up in the 1960s, I spent those magical weeks before Christmas in a state of near rapture, marveling at the splendor of our deluxe aluminum Christmas tree. This feat of modern electronics came complete with rotating base and alternating color-wheel floodlights. The effect was dazzling—a glistening, icelike tower that spun slowly on its axis, its shiny branches bouncing colored beams of light against the walls like the starburst reflections of a dance-hall mirror ball. In the background, the *Andy Williams Christmas Album* offered stereophonic wishes of a snowy Yuletide visit from Santa Claus. Every square inch of our home was obsessively embellished with beaded stockings, sequined Santas, glittering garlands, and snowy village vignettes. My mother, the Queen of Christmas—normally a woman of impeccable taste—was transformed by the Christmas spirit into a slave to all things shiny. Our holiday living room looked like a Vegas floor show, and I adored it. This technicolor time of year was the backdrop for the happiest of my childhood memories.

For young and old alike, Christmas is a vacation in upside-down town. For a child, nothing is the same as it is the rest of the year. Parents are more playful and the house is filled with music, toys, candy, and all the pie you can eat. For adults, Christmas is the time when a strange transformation takes place. Our sophisticated conventions fly out the window and tasteful color palettes are replaced with Santa Suit red, Christmas Tree green, and anything that glitters. We festoon formerly pristine walls in greenery and hammer twisted strings of light into place with reckless abandon until the entire house sparkles like a float in a holiday parade. Are we finally owning up to our basic lack of taste? Perhaps. But more likely, we're just caught up in the childlike magic of Christmas and all things kitsch. And why not? 'Tis the season to be kitschy. At no other time of the year is there such a collective lapse in taste and good judgment. The flocked trees, the useless trinkets, the Santa wrapping paper, the monumental pile of gifts, the magical snowmen and reindeer that sing . . . you don't have to look far to see that we all lose our minds when it comes to Kitschmas. Some say it's gone too far. But I say, "Rubbish! It hasn't gone far enough!"

That's where this book comes in. *Merry Kitschmas* is a no-holds-barred extravaganza of kitschy Christmas inspiration—your guide to stretching the boundaries of your own good taste and really letting your creative freak flag fly! With wacky wreaths, tacky trinkets, campy couture, and so much more, this book will help you really dive into the Kitschmas spirit. So give in to the magic, the mayhem, and the mania. Throw on a pair of stretch pants, down that third helping of pie, and set your glue gun to extra hot. Kitschmas time is sparkly, it's silly, and, as Andy Williams put it, "It's the most wonderful time of the year!"

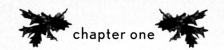

chapter one

Oh, Kitschmas Tree, Oh KitschmasTree!

ike many traditions gone haywire, the customary Christmas tree began innocently. In Europe, long before the Christian era, branches of evergreen brightened dreary homes through the long, cold winters. The first freshly cut holiday tree probably entered the home as a German *Paradeisbaum,* or Paradise tree—a symbol of the Garden of Eden. These trees were simply adorned with apples, establishing the red and green colors traditional to the season. The modest *Paradeisbaum* evolved into the fancier *Tannenbaum,* a rather gaudy number embellished with shiny tin decorations, candy, cookies, and the perplexingly hazardous addition of lit candles. Prince Albert later imported the trend to England, where ornament-obsessed Victorians constructed toy-, fruit-, and candy-laden fantasias for their holiday festivities. Eventually, the traditional Christmas tree came to America, where it became the flocked, tinseled, electrified, aluminized, glitterized, and plasticized extravaganza we know and love. Here lies the very essence of Kitschmas— another humble tradition skidding down a glitter-slicked highway into a wreckage of tasteless and fabulous abandon.

A stunning tree is the center-stage superstar of any Kitschmastime spectacular. This ruling diva of the holidays demands the most attention, the best lighting, all the gifts, and branchloads of sparkling baubles. Like most epic theatrical productions, Kitschmas is built around its charismatic star. (In some homes, she's even known to play out a dramatic death scene in the final act.) Casting your own magnificent tree is where your Kitschmas extravaganza begins.

In the following pages you'll find suggestions and starting points for creating your own Kitschmas tree fantasy. Don't be timid. No one else is! As long as there are malls to shop in, there will be gaudier trees than yours out there to behold. As the legendary Broadway diva, Ethel Merman once belted, "Curtain up! Light the lights! You've got nothin' to hit but the heights!"

Kitsch it up a notch with this decorative and delectable Weenie Tree (page 29), perfect for your next swanky Kitschmas cocktail party.

I'M DREAMING OF A
white-trash Kitschmas

* * *

You haven't experienced Kitschmas until you've driven through a trailer park in December. The creativity! The resourceful use of tinfoil and duct tape! The elaborately decorated vehicles on blocks in the front yard! Can't you hear the dueling banjos and smell Ellie May's biscuits a-burnin' on the stove? For those of us running just as fast as we can from our inner white-trash child, hoping no one will notice the powdered sugar in the corners of our mouths or the gravy stains on our shirts, this is the perfect Kitschmas tree. Still, one needn't be white, poor, or trash to celebrate the painfully unsophisticated side in all of us.

This monochromatic dream of a tree is decorated with powdered doughnuts, shiny mud-flap gals, duct-tape bows, cotton-swab snowflakes, and small hors d'oeuvres crackers that look remarkably like tiny slices of white bread. As the shining star of trash, the tree is topped by the classic aerodynamic design of a toy Airstream. So assemble your common-law family on the front porch couch and sing, "May your days be merry and bright, and may all your Kitschmases be white… trash!"

YOU WILL NEED

1 white artificial tabletop Christmas tree
White twinkle lights with white cord
White yarn
12 mini powdered-sugar doughnuts
Hot-glue gun and glue sticks
40 cotton swabs
Small craft paintbrush
Iridescent glitter glue
Silver thread
20 mini toasts (crackers that look like tiny white bread slices, for example Le Petit Pain Grillé brand)
Doll needle (thick, long, and strong)
"Mud Honey"

1 Set up your tree and decorate with the twinkle lights.

2 Using the white yarn, string the doughnuts and hang on the tree.

3 Hot-glue 4 cotton swabs together in an asterisk-like formation to create a delicate snowflake. With the craft brush, paint on a little glitter glue to give it a little frosty sparkle. Hang with silver thread. Repeat until you have 10 finished snowflakes hanging.

4 Line up 20 mini toasts and squirt each with glitter glue, like a dollop of mayonnaise. When dry, punch a hole near the top of each with the doll needle. Hang on the tree with silver thread.

5 Remove one of the "Mud Honeys" from your truck, and place it onto a copy machine. Enlarge or reduce her to a suitable size. Cut loosely around

Scissors
Tape
Silver cardboard (high-gloss "mirror board")
Ballpoint pen
X-Acto knife
Duct tape
Wire ornament hangers
1 can of white spray paint
One ⅜-inch wooden dowel rod cut to 15 inches long
1 miniature Airstream trailer (check the Internet)
1 used CD
18 inches of floral wire

shape to remove excess paper. Tape the paper onto your silver cardboard and trace the outline of the shape, using a ballpoint pen with enough pressure to transfer an indentation to the next layer. Using the X-Acto knife, cut out the shape. With a needle and silver thread, punch through the cardboard to make a loop, and hang on the tree. Repeat 4 more times to get 5 mud-flap femme fatales.

6 Cut the duct tape into a 12-inch strip. On a flat surface, carefully fold the tape in half, sticky-sides together, trying to avoid unsightly wrinkles. You now have a 2-by-6-inch piece of double-thick duct tape that has no exposed adhesive. Cut a ½-inch strip along the 6-inch length and set aside. Fold the larger piece in half and pinch it in the center to create a nice bow-tie shape. Using the thin strip, tie a single knot around the pinched area, arranging it into a nice traditional holiday bow, trimming the ends to your preference. Repeat as many times as you like, and attach to the tree with wire ornament hangers.

7 Spray-paint the dowel rod white and allow to dry. Hot-glue the miniature Airstream to the silvery side of the CD and let cool. Turn the trailer/CD upside down, exposing the center hole of the CD. Put a little hot glue in the center hole and insert the dowel, holding it until the glue is cool and the dowel is secure. Strengthen the joint with a second layer of hot glue, holding it in place until it cools. Place the Airstream tree-topper in place by running the dowel rod down the center of the tree, attaching it by winding the floral wire around it and the tree's central "trunk."

BONUS IDEA! Wrap your presents using want ads, foil, tabloid scandal magazines, candy wrappers, plastic bread bags, eviction notices, warrants, restraining orders, and lotto tickets to make the look complete.

HAPPY HULADAYS
tree

✶ ✶ ✶

While some dream of a white-trash Kitschmas, others have been snowbound in a frost-bitten city for weeks and are in desperate need of escaping to a tropical island. Well, put on your flowered shirt, your grass skirt, and the *Don Ho Christmas Album,* it's time to make a Polynesian paradise!

There is a tidal wave of decorations for adorning this tree. Since the Hawaiian craze swept across the American pop culture scene during the forties, fifties, and sixties, almost everything Hawaiian smacks of kitsch. From dashboard hula dancers to light-up tiki gods, American novelty manufacturers went coconuts for anything tropical. The trick with this tree is to pick and choose so that you're making a somewhat focused statement—otherwise your tree will look like a lunatic's luau. This wiki-wacky tree spotlights the hypnotic and sensual hula, Hawaii's quintessential native dance. It will warm your huladays like a week in Waikiki. Who knows, you might even get lei'd!

✳ ✳ ✳

1   Tie the loose ends of the tomato cage together with twist ties to create a Christmas tree-shaped frame.

2   With a twist tie, hang one corner of the tree skirt to the tomato cage so that the end of the grass barely touches the ground. Begin to wrap the table skirt around and up the cage, slowly working your way up to cover the cage completely, securing the opposite end of the skirt to the top of the cage with another twist tie.

3   Arrange your light strings around the tree, in an even coverage, securing them onto the tomato cage frame with twist ties.

4   Drape the tree with leis as you would a tinsel garland.

5   Fill in any sparse areas with cocktail parasols, or various festive ornaments.

6   Top the tree with the dashboard hula dancer to get the luau started.

Mele Kalikimaka me ka Hau'oli Makahiki Hou!

VALLEY OF THE DOLLS
tree

* * *

Your plastic fashion dolls sprang from the box looking like fresh-faced Hollywood starlets, but two weeks in your frantic, ten-year-old grip and they ended up naked, dirty, and sporting a hairdo fit for a sanitarium. These dolls of Kitschmas past have been through the wringer and are in desperate need of a glitzy comeback. Bring them front and center again in this masterpiece of kitsch, an homage to one of the worst movies ever made and a gentle reminder of the exhilarating highs and desperate lows of fast-lane fame. For extra inspiration, rent the video, if only to see Patty and Susan duke it out in the ladies' room. It just ain't a good cat fight unless someone's wig ends up in the can!

YOU WILL NEED

10 old, used fashion dolls
1 can of gray spray primer
1 can of silver spray paint
1 bottle of silver chrome nail polish
Fine-detail craft paintbrush
1 container black model paint
1 container pink model paint
White drafting tape
X-Acto knife
Scissors
½ yard silver lamé fabric
Hot-glue gun (one with a low-heat setting) and low-melt glue sticks
Iridescent glitter glue
One 10-inch-tall-by-6-inch-wide galvanized steel floral bucket
Bolt cutter or tin snips
One 12-inch round metal serving tray
1 premade 6-by-12-inch topiary form with a 4-inch trunk and a 3-inch base (available at most craft stores)
1 battery-operated twinkle microlight set (20 lights)

1　Start by gathering all your daughter's old, tattered fashion dolls and removing their heads; set the heads aside. Spray all the bodies with a series of light layers of primer, allowing each layer to dry between applications. When the primer is completely dry, spray the bodies with the silver paint.

2　Paint the faces of the doll heads with the nail polish, being careful not to cover the eyes. Using the fine-detail brush, paint heavy eyeliner and brows on all the doll heads with the black model paint, and paint the lips with the pink paint. Put their heads back on and fix their hair—for cryin' out loud, they look awful!

3　Line them up and pick the most glamorous of the bunch. Put her aside, as she will now be the fabulous star of this show (the others must dance in the chorus). Now comes the cruel part, and a testimonial to how rotten this business really is: choose the doll that is the least beautiful, rip every limb from her body, and toss her aside, too, to use for parts in the final act (step 10).

4　As a salute to Neely O'Hara's drunken, midnight swim, dress the dolls in unflattering bras and slips. Using the drafting tape, make big, white,

Floral pins

Duct Tape

Assorted candies that look like
prescription medication

1 empty prescription bottle

Novelty miniature Champagne bottles
and glasses (available where they sell
wedding party supplies)

✳ ✳ ✳

pointy, vintage-looking brassieres: place strips of tape directly onto the
dolls and trim them to shape using the X-Acto knife (oh, don't be naive,
this isn't the first time they've gone under the knife in the name of beauty).
With the scissors, cut the lamé into 3-by-5-inch strips and make a fast slip
by hot-gluing everything in place, not worrying about how the backs look,
since no one will see them. Add a little glitter glue to the bras, and "Sparkle
Neely, Sparkle!"

5   Hot-glue the gals, shoulder to shoulder, around the floral bucket. Be
sure to use low-melt glue sticks and have your hot-glue gun on the low-
heat setting; you don't want your dolls to melt! Once in place, the dolls
will be longer than the bucket, so align the tops of their heads with the top
edge of the bucket, and trim their legs with the bolt cutter or tin snips to be
even with the base.

6   Hot-glue the girl-clad bucket to the center of the serving tray. Then
glue the topiary form in the center of the bucket with plenty of hot glue.

7   Position the microlights on the foam cone using floral pins. When you
are satisfied with the placement of each light, cover all the wires, pins, and
the topiary form's surface with strips of duct tape, leaving only the lights
exposed. Hot-glue the battery pack to the underside of the cone near the
back, so it is not easily seen.

8   Choosing from your variety of candies, begin hot-gluing them to the
tape-covered cone. Create a pattern of your liking, covering the entire
cone surface and working around the lights.

9   Take the "star" of this show (step 3) and break her in half at the waist
(fame doesn't come easy). Hot glue her into the top of the tree, as if she is
wearing a huge dress made entirely of barbiturates and amphetamines.

10   Fill the tray and the top of the bucket with candy "pills," adding the
prescription bottle, the doll parts, and a few miniature Champagne bottles
and glasses to give the dramatic look of a liquor-soaked swinger party
gone terribly wrong. After this, you might want to check into a sanitarium
to dry out.

HANDY HIS-AND-HER
tree

* * *

This "handy" tree is inspired by holiday housekeeping magazines from the 1950s, which filled virtually every page with glossy how-to's that promised a splendid Yuletide celebration and showed husbands and wives playing their roles to their holiday hilt. Smiling ladies took charge of festive interior decorations, crafty kid projects, and mouthwatering meals showcasing some of the million-and-one things to do with gelatin. Cheerful men shouldered the burden of the outdoor yard projects, lighting extravaganzas, anything that required a power tool, and the honored task of carving the family turkey (the women could rip the guts out and stuff the sucker, but they were far too delicate to handle a big scary knife in front of company).

The his-and-her tree illustrates traditional family values like a split-screen scene from a Rock Hudson–Doris Day comedy. His side is made of green garden gloves for those blustery December dusks, testing tangled light strings in the front yard. Her side is made of bright yellow latex gloves to protect her soft and supple hands from the drudgery of holiday housework. Decorations made from gender-specific toys and advertising images add the finishing touches.

YOU WILL NEED

Protective eyewear, thick gloves, and long sleeves
One 4-by-5-foot sheet of 23-gauge, ¼-inch galvanized hardware cloth (metal fencing, available at hardware stores)
Tin snips
20 gauge floral wire
Fat-tipped marker
String
Duct tape
80 pairs men's green garden gloves
80 pairs ladies' yellow latex household gloves
8 pounds polyester fiberfill
Crochet hook

1 Making the large cone-shaped cage is best done with two people wearing protective eyewear, thick gloves, and long sleeves. Make a large cone shape with the hardware cloth, like you would make a paper funnel, except on a REALLY BIG scale. When you get the desired shape and height, trim any excess with the tin snips and sew the edges of the doubled areas with floral wire with one person stiching the cone while the other person holds it, being careful not to lose the shape.

2 Tie the marker to the end of a piece of string that is a little longer than the desired height of the tree. Have one person hold the string at the point of the funnel as the other person runs a mark around the tree, being careful to keep the string straight. With the tin snips, cut along the marked area. Cover the rough edge with duct tape to guard against injury.

Scanned images from vintage magazines
Spray adhesive or glue stick
Poster or foam board
X-Acto knife
Ornament hooks
20 feet of small-link chain
20 feet of prestrung pearls
Assorted "girl"-specific miniaturized
　　household-themed toys
Assorted "boy"-specific miniaturized
　　tool-themed toys
1 male action figure, dressed in
　　workman's overalls
1 female fashion doll, dressed as a '50s
　　housewife
Spray glitter

NOTE
Be very careful to keep your ornaments
on the correct side of the tree or no one
will know what to do, what to wear, or
how to act, and Kitschmas as we know it
will be ruined forever.

✳ ✳ ✳

3 Stuff the green and yellow gloves with the polyester fiberfill, starting with the fingers and then the hands. Do not pack them too full. They should have a loose, floppy look.

4 With the marker, draw straight lines on the front and back of the tree form, dividing it in half.

5 Cut 320 pieces of 4-inch floral wire lengths.

6 Starting at the bottom of the wire-mesh tree form, begin attaching the gloves with wire, piercing through the gloves and the mesh, pulling the ends back through using the crochet hook, and twisting off the ends. Arrange the gloves to cover fully and have a nice balance of colors. Repeat until you have a tree of gloves.

7 Enlarge vintage advertising images using a desktop scanner and printer or a color copy machine. Using the spray adhesive, mount the images to the poster board. Carefully cut out the images with the X-Acto knife, and hang on the tree with ornament hooks.

8 Drape the chain on the green side and the pearls on the yellow, as you would a tinsel garland. Secure the ends at strategic peak points to the gloves using wire.

9 Place the male action figure and female fashion doll atop the tree, securing them in place with wire.

10 Add ornament hooks to the minature toys and hang on the tree.

11 Spray the whole tree with a light dusting of spray glitter, shine a bright light on it, and watch it glisten.

THE TREE
of the future

* * *

Throughout the twentieth century, visionaries predicted a fantastic future in space, void of anything natural, organic, or remotely comfortable, where humans lived a lifestyle perfected by science. These visions inspired designers to boldly go where no one had gone before, and many of their designs became kitsch classics, beloved by sci-fi enthusiasts and loft–living modernists alike. Did you ever get an elementary school writing assignment to imagine "life in the future"? Well, here's a tree for your futuristic imaginings, using materials readily available to schoolchildren everywhere. This ghost of Kitschmas future is much more fun than a Dickensian trip through a graveyard. You can almost hear HAL calling, "Dave, It's Kitschmas. Time to put up the tree."

YOU WILL NEED

Protective eyewear
One 39-by-48-inch white plastic canvas (found in stores that sell rug-hooking supplies)
Tin snips
Silver floral wire
Fat-tipped marker
String
Hot-glue gun (one with a low-heat setting) and LOTS of low-melt hot-glue sticks
About 500 white 3-ounce plastic cups
1 ultramodern light tree star
1 table lamp with lampshade
1 light bulb, no more than 45 watts

1 Making the large cone-shaped cage is best done with two people wearing protective eyewear. Make a large cone shape with the plastic canvas, like you would make a paper funnel, except on a REALLY BIG scale. When you get the desired shape and height, trim away any excess canvas with the tin snips and sew the edges of the doubled areas with floral wire, with one person stitching the cone while the other person holds it, being careful not to lose the shape.

2 Tie the marker to the end of a piece of string that is a little longer than the desired height of the tree. Have one person hold the string at the point of the funnel as the other person runs a mark around the tree, being careful to keep the string straight.

∗ ∗ ∗

3   With the tin snips, cut along the marked area.

4   Set the hot-glue gun to a low setting. Begin to hot-glue the cups to the tree form, one at a time, starting at the top. You will want to start on one side to get the hang of it (the first side will probably face the wall). The idea is to get the cups as close together as possible.

5   Drop your groovy, ultramod light tree star's cord down through the top and secure the star by hot-gluing it in place.

6   Screw the lightbulb into the table lamp. Place your table lamp where you would like the tree to be, pick up the cup-covered tree, and place it carefully over the lamp (shade and all), making sure that nothing touches the lightbulb.

JINGLE BALL
and weenie trees

✳ ✳ ✳

Planning a swanky adult Kitschmas Kocktail shindig? Try these perfect timesaving, crowd-pleasing multipurpose trees. They're decorative! They're edible! They're delicious cheese balls, meatballs, or whatever balls! There is a rich legacy of holiday ball recipes. For some unknown reason, ladies from the fifties were obsessed with balls and weenies. If you don't have a bunch of ball recipes, call your mom; most likely she has tons of them! Be warned, some people are very funny about their balls. Some of these top secret recipes have been carefully protected like the family jewels. So don't go around asking just anyone to show you theirs; they may not be so accommodating.

What would a Jingle Ball Tree be without its obligatory companion, the classic Weenie Tree (photo, page 12), made with heat-and-serve cocktail wieners. Oddly, they seem to go hand in hand, like a matching set. Go forth and multiply this recipe as needed for bigger parties or a thickly treed festive forest.

✳ ✳ ✳

YOU WILL NEED

Two 1-quart plastic containers
Plaster of paris
Two ⅜-by-11-inch wooden dowel rods
Masking tape
Two 12-by-4-inch Styrofoam cone forms
Aluminum foil or shiny gift wrap
Double-stick tape
Hot-glue gun and hot-glue sticks
Scraps of felt
Ribbon
Bric-a-brac
Food balls of your choice
Cocktail weenies
Toothpicks

1 It is best to prepare your tree forms an hour or two in advance, so the plaster of paris is dry enough to hold the dowel rod firmly (it will be fully dry in 24 hours). Fill a plastic container three-fourths full with plaster of paris mixed according to package directions. Place a wooden dowel in the center to make the trunk. Using the precut masking tape strips, make a series of stabilizing straps across the rim of the can. Double-check to make sure it is plumb before allowing it to set. Let dry completely. Repeat with second container and dowel.

2 When the plaster base is dry, push a Styrofoam cone onto each dowel and cover the cones with aluminum foil or gift wrap. Use double-stick tape to close the seam. Trim any excess paper.

3 Using the hot-glue gun and glue sticks, decorate the plastic container with felt, ribbons, and bric-a-brac to give it that sixties swing.

4 Prepare your balls and weenies. Arrange the balls on one tree and the weenies on the other, using toothpicks to attach them to the Styrofoam.

5 Whew! You must be thirsty—time for cocktails!

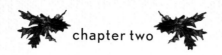

chapter two

Deck the Halls
(and Walls and Doors and Floors)
with Lotsa Tchotchkes!
Fa, la, la, la, la, la, la, la, la

Now that you have your spectacular Kitschmas tree, it's time to harmonize the rest of your home with snazzy symbols of the season. If not, your tree could stand out like a hooker at a PTA meeting. From the wreath that welcomes your guests at the door to the stockings hung by the hearth with care, your obsessive attention to detail will let everyone know that you are full of it—the Kitschmas spirit, that is.

The kitsch motto is: Leave no table untopped. Look around you; there are a thousand surfaces waiting to fulfill their Kitschmas destiny. The top of your mega-screen TV is calling out for a gingerbread nativity scene. You could give yours wide-open stable doors and call out, "Jesus, were ya born in a barn?" Or, you could create a modern table-top Bedford Falls, the idyllic small town from *It's a Wonderful Life*. Imagine it in today's world of apartments, strip malls, chain retailers, Starbucks, and convenience stores. Title it, "It's a Hideous Suburban Life" and call it a day. In this chapter, you'll find ideas for kitschy wreaths, outlandish exterior lighting projects, stockings with a twist, and more. Hang up your lights and swag your garlands. Don't hide your light under a bushel! It's Kitschmas for crying out loud, this is your chance to shine.

◁ **The perfect wreath for RV enthusiasts or people who just don't give a crap.**

KITSCHMAS
wreaths

* * *

Wreaths are the ultimate holiday doornament. A beautifully decorated portal is your home's first design statement and a hint of things to come. Whether made of freshly cut greenery, dried berries, or a durable synthetic, a wreath can be an elegant welcome to any home, setting the tone for a lovely Yuletide visit. But this is Kitschmas, and elegant wreaths can hang themselves on every other tract-house door on the block. There are better ways to go when it comes to wreaths. From the glitzy and complicated to the RIDICULOUSLY simple, the following wreath ideas offer a range of choices, or may spark a blizzard-like brainstorm of your own to suitably reflect your unique holly, jolly, folly this Kitschmas season.

PAGE 32   **Too Tired Wreath**

This wreath speaks to the straight-C student in all of us. All you need is an old flat tire (that you've needed to get rid of for years anyway), wire to hang it, and some duct tape to make a quick and easy bow. You're tired, your time is precious, and you don't want to miss any of your favorite reality shows. Remember to take it down sometime in the spring, before it gets too hot. If you forget, just leave it up until next year.

OPPOSITE   **Have Your Elves a Merry Little Kitschmas Wreath**

This little retro wreath breathes new life into those impish ornaments that have littered many a tree for decades. This particular group of rubber elf heads came from a set of vintage tree lights, but these characters were commonly seen in many different kinds of Kitschmas novelties. Gather a bunch of them from the attic or your local thrift store and wire them onto an existing holiday wreath. This project is a great example of recycling relics from the past into new kitschy classics. Surprisingly, the power of repetition transforms these normally benevolent characters from sprightly to spiteful when gathered together in a gang of potentially mischievous pixies, producing a wreath with an edge.

* * *

A Wreath of Franklins

The perfect way to dress your threshold if you happen to be a fan (and who isn't?) of the undisputed Queen of Soul. Start with a large photo of Miss Aretha herself, then make your wreath by giving her a halo of one-hundred-dollar bills, all pinned to a Styrofoam wreath form. Of course, the tricky part is getting your mitts on five thousand dollars' worth of Ben Franklins. If need be, pound the pavement and take up a collection. At your holiday party, serenade your guests with her majesty's classic rendition of "Winter Wonderland" to make your statement complete. You will get plenty of R.E.S.P.E.C.T. now that your guests see how rich you are. Sock it to me, sock it to me, sock it to me. . . .

The Urban Legend Fruitcake Wreath

What would Kitschmas be without a scary fruitcake in the mail? Urban legend holds that a mere handful of fruitcakes are passed around from season to season like holiday hot potatoes. This wreath pays homage to the fruitcake of urban lore and, even better, it lasts forever at room temperature. Actually, we would suggest you use a real fruitcake, but since the weight of it might take your door down, this lighter faux creation will be far less hazardous to your home. This one's easy: start with a Styrofoam wreath form, cover it with clay, and stud it with pecans. What a welcome!

BERRY WHITE
wreath

✳ ✳ ✳

Ohhhh Baby! What a dyn-o-mite way to greet your guests and hip them to the solid fact that you are a swingin' love maestro who is clearly qualified to sa-tis-fy. Perfect for bachelor pads, old-school dance-music enthusiasts, or those just stuck in the late seventies. It is also a fabulous way to pay tribute to the voice that launched a million horizontal hustles. The secret to this eye-catching wreath is that absolutely nothing is real or intended to look natural. It's all about flash, glitz, and low-down looooooove.

YOU WILL NEED

10 yards of 2 ½-inch white satin bridal ribbon
One 12-inch white Styrofoam wreath form
Straight pins
2 strings of battery-operated white holiday microlights (white cords as well)
Tape measure
Pencil
Floral wire
About fifteen hundred 8-mm pearl beads
Hot-glue gun and tons of hot-glue sticks
Twenty-nine 1 ½-inch Styrofoam mirror-ball ornaments
One 9-inch round piece of very thin craft acrylic (like thin Plexiglas)
Tape
Wax paper
Sculpey polymer craft clay
1 can of silver spray paint
About 150 small, faceted fake gemstones
Good-quality gem glue such as Aleene's
One 4-inch Styrofoam mirror-ball ornament

1 Using the white satin ribbon, wrap the entire wreath: anchor the end with a few straight pins, and wrap at an angle. Keep a fairly tight tension on the ribbon to make a smooth surface.

2 Using the tape measure and pencil, place each light every 2 inches or so around the wreath. Secure each light in place with floral wire.

3 Mount the battery packs on the back of the wreath. Pin all the loose wire out of sight on the back of the wreath.

4 Start the never-ending placement of the berrylike pearl beads with generous amounts of hot glue. Be careful, you will undoubtedly burn yourself a thousand times, like I did.

5 Bead the entire front surface of the wreath and the sides of the center hole. Continue to bead halfway down the outside edges, leaving room to place the small mirror balls.

6 Center the acrylic circle on the back of the wreath and hot-glue it into place.

✳ ✳ ✳

7 Run a 6-inch piece of floral wire through each small mirror ball. Use the ends of the wires and more hot glue to attach them securely to the perimeter of the wreath.

8 Using the photo (facing page) for inspiration, create an "Oh Baby" graphic. Tape it to a work surface and tape a sheet of wax paper over it. Using the graphic as a guide, form your Sculpey in the shape of the words. This is supposed to look like a big version of those seventies necklaces that said things like "Foxy" or "Babe." Using the tip of your little finger or the eraser of a pencil, make a bunch of dents in the surface of the Sculpey letters to hold each gemstone. Bake according to the directions on the Sculpey package. When cooked and cooled, spray-paint the finished pieces silver. Affix each gemstone in the dents you made with gem glue. Finally, hot-glue "Oh Baby" into position on the acrylic backing. It will look like it is magically floating on air.

9 Pin the 4-inch mirror ball to the bottom of the wreath and secure with floral wire, as shown.

10 Plug in the eight-track, dim the lights, and splash on a little aftershave. It's time for love.

HE SEES YOU WHEN YOU'RE SLEEPING
night-light

* * *

It's hard to tell if the lyricist of "Santa Claus Is Coming to Town" was a genius or a sadistic jokester. One thing is for sure, the line "He sees you when you're sleeping" is a mean seed for nighttime anxiety attacks, paranoia, and sleepless hours of searching for the hidden camera (if Allen Funt could hide a camera, why not Santa?). Small price to pay for a few weeks of good behavior from the young and impressionable, though. If your rug rat isn't buying this story, create this night-light, almost guaranteed to keep little ones in line. Suggest that the light sensor at the bottom of the night-light is a lens AND a microphone. It's a gift that keeps on giving (hours of fun on the shrink's couch later in life!). Plug this baby in, turn out the lights, and sing softly, "You better watch out!"

YOU WILL NEED

Scissors

Any old plastic doll head of a scale suitable to your night-light

Sculpey polymer craft clay in red and white

1 ovenproof glass bowl

About 2 cups of uncooked rice

X-Acto knife

Hot-glue gun and glue sticks

Fine-tip black marker

Good-quality white craft glue such as Aleene's Tacky Glue

White and red seed beads (optional)

1 standard night-light with sensor (get one with a good plastic lens to prevent anything from touching the bulb—use your own good sense here and don't burn your house down, for cryin' out loud!)

1 Using scissors, gently cut your doll head in half (discard the back portion of the little head ASAP–it looks creepy).

2 Roll out your red and white Sculpey into shapes.

3 Assemble the whole thing on the doll head to create Santa. Sculpt your little heart out. When you are satisfied with your creation, move on to step 4.

4 Put the whole thing in the freezer and let it sit for a few hours.

5 Carefully remove the clay from the doll head (since the clay is frozen, this should be a lot easier, but use a gentle touch or you may have to go back to step 2 and start over with fresh clay).

6 Polymer clay tends to change shape during baking, so I devised a way to prevent this: Fill an ovenproof bowl halfway with rice. Gently place the clay pieces on the rice and push and rock gently to tuck them into the rice. Do not let the pieces touch one another. Bake according to directions on the Sculpey package. Let cool.

7 While the clay is baking and cooling, wash off any residual clay from the doll head. Now is a good time to do a little eye surgery. This step is not for the squeamish. With your X-Acto knife, cut out the eyes (all dolls are not created equal, but most eyes can be cut free by removing the back of the plastic socket). The idea is to move the eyes into a more intense, maniacal position, i.e., looking down with the whites showing above the iris. When you like the look in your Santa's eyes, hot-glue them in place.

8 Draw a little eyeliner with the fine-tip marker to accentuate Santa's "Norma Desmond" glare.

9 When all your clay elements have cooled, hot-glue the pieces in place.

10 Bead the hat with craft glue and seed beads. (You can skip this step if you are of the "less is more" school—but then again, if you were, why would you even be doing this?)

11 Hot-glue the head to the night-light.

12 Sing "Santa Claus Is Coming to Town," turn out the lights, and put a little money aside for later therapy.

He sees you when you're sleeping
He knows when you're awake
He knows if you've been bad or good
So be good for goodness' sake

★ J. Fred Coots & Henry Gillespie

NAUGHTY AND NICE
stockings

* * *

The traditional stocking hung by the chimney with care seems to have originated with a legendary holiday tale of woe. One version of the story tells of a kindly nobleman who, having fallen into desperate poverty, was grief stricken that his three daughters, renowned for their goodness, were too poor to marry. One night, after the sisters washed their only stockings, hanging them by the fire to dry, and retiring to bed, Saint Nicholas, who had been touched by their sad tale, peeped into the window, saw the stockings, and got a brilliant idea. He leapt to the chimney and threw three bags of gold down the flu, magically landing in each girl's stocking, giving birth to the holiday fable of a saintly old man bestowing gifts to good-hearted underdogs.

This spoken legend spread like a distorted rumor throughout Europe and spawned many different variations on the tradition of holiday stockings. One peculiar version evolved into the Dutch tale of Sinterklaas, who after a year of spying on children, rewarded good youngsters with a bounty of gifts and candy, while bad kids were left with onions, coal, or switches. Harsh? Perhaps. But it proves that parenting has not changed much through the ages. Using Santa Claus as an underhanded discipline shortcut didn't start with our poor, frazzled mothers—it started centuries ago.

Now, for these enlightened times, we present the following stocking ideas for modern characters and new definitions that lie between those old concepts of good and bad, naughty and nice, for young and old alike. Or let these inspire you to invent your own. Either way, hang with pride, and stuff the stockings with lighthearted gifts to remind the recipients of their good or bad conduct throughout the year.

LEFT **The Bad Girl's Ho Ho Ho Stocking**
Made from a red vinyl fetish boot for those adult girrrrrrls who know that being naughty is sometimes nice.

CENTER **The Manipulative Parent's Reversible Stocking**
A super holiday tool and a new way to control the children. Threaten to hang the stocking naughty-side out unless they do everything you tell them to. Ah, the Joy of the Holidays!

RIGHT **NASDAQ Stock-ing**
For the bad dad who invested the kid's education fund in tech stocks. Velcro seams insure that the stocking falls apart when it gets too full. Perfect for the guy who had everything!

THE JUDY
garland

✳ ✳ ✳

The garland is a classic holiday decorating staple that brightens your home inside and out. If you are looking for a glitzy way to frame your threshold, try this glamorous, Technicolor version. When used as a door embellishment, it greets your guests with an "over the top" trip under the rainbow, setting the tone for a memorable holiday gathering. It can also be utilized as a show-stopping interior decor item when placed strategically for cocktail parties. If your life resembles an MGM musical (and whose doesn't?), hang or drape your garland within arm's distance in the event of a spontaneous song. You might want to keep a video camera at the ready to capture a drunken rendition of "Have Yourself a Merry Little Christmas." There's just something about feather boas, a couple of eggnoggs, and a Judy Garland classic to coax the holiday hams out of the closet.

This project is very easy because you don't have to make the boa. The trick is in finding out where to get them. The best sources are found through online retail sites that specialize in costumes or exotic playwear.

YOU WILL NEED

Small, nonbreakable, plastic ornaments in a rainbow of colors

A number of 6-foot rainbow-striped turkey feather boas

Needle and thread

Jingle bells

1 Securely attach the plastic ornaments along the length of the boa using the needle and thread (it's best to sew them in case someone actually gets drunk and/or carried away and flings it around).

2 Sew the bells on the ends of the garland for a little extra jingle and swing when someone throws it over their shoulder.

3 Hang, swag, or drape to your heart's content.

NOTE

It is not recommended to use plug-in lights to decorate these garlands, as turkey feathers smell truly hideous when they burn.

NO ROOM AT THE INN
lighting extravaganza

* * *

Exterior holiday decoration has historically been the exclusive territory of the family menfolk (see Handy His-and-Her Tree, page 23, for further chauvinistic thoughts). Gals, this need not be the case! However, you must be forewarned of the playing field you are about to step onto. If the cleats don't fit, you might want to sit this one out on the bench. Men have turned front-yard decorating into a competitive, extreme sport. It has nothing to do with beauty, harmony, or design. It is all about wattage, size, height, and the level of power-tool difficulty, the principal objective being: outdo every other player on the block. This is one of the few times a manly man will show any interest at all in the fanciful world of decorating, so you might want to leave good enough alone. This is the decorating Superbowl! Let them play their reindeer games—at least it will get them up off the couch for a while!

We present this macho, front-yard lighting extravaganza in the language of blueprint, void of any sissy shopping lists, directives, or helpful hints. Understanding blueprints and scale models puts the test in testosterone. This brain-stem skill taps into two things that men do very well: the ability to imagine things much bigger than they actually are, and staring at models. If you aren't up for the challenge, hit the showers, you pantywaist! You're out of your league!

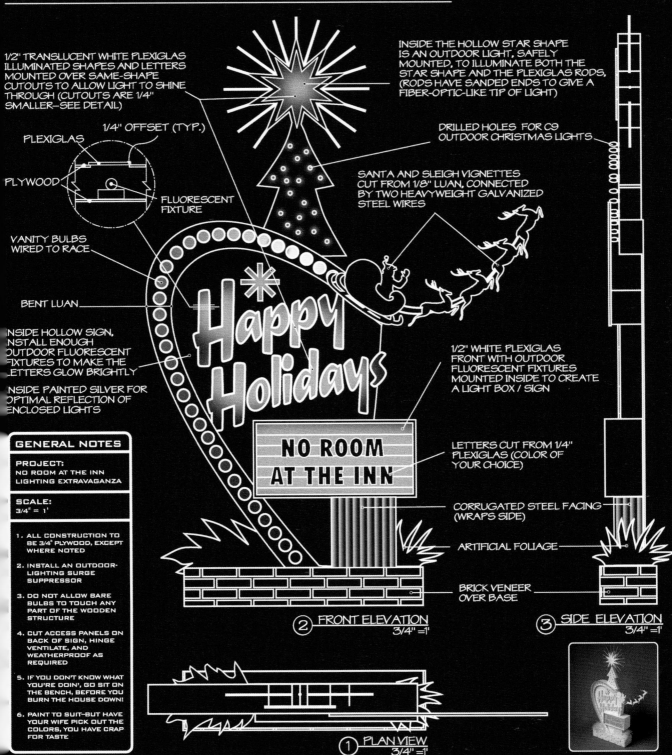

1/2" TRANSLUCENT WHITE PLEXIGLAS ILLUMINATED SHAPES AND LETTERS MOUNTED OVER SAME-SHAPE CUTOUTS TO ALLOW LIGHT TO SHINE THROUGH (CUTOUTS ARE 1/4" SMALLER—SEE DETAIL)

INSIDE THE HOLLOW STAR SHAPE IS AN OUTDOOR LIGHT, SAFELY MOUNTED, TO ILLUMINATE BOTH THE STAR SHAPE AND THE PLEXIGLAS RODS, (RODS HAVE SANDED ENDS TO GIVE A FIBER-OPTIC-LIKE TIP OF LIGHT)

1/4" OFFSET (TYP.)

PLEXIGLAS

PLYWOOD

FLUORESCENT FIXTURE

DRILLED HOLES FOR C9 OUTDOOR CHRISTMAS LIGHTS

SANTA AND SLEIGH VIGNETTES CUT FROM 1/8" LUAN, CONNECTED BY TWO HEAVYWEIGHT GALVANIZED STEEL WIRES

VANITY BULBS WIRED TO RACE

BENT LUAN

INSIDE HOLLOW SIGN, INSTALL ENOUGH OUTDOOR FLUORESCENT FIXTURES TO MAKE THE LETTERS GLOW BRIGHTLY

INSIDE PAINTED SILVER FOR OPTIMAL REFLECTION OF ENCLOSED LIGHTS

1/2" WHITE PLEXIGLAS FRONT WITH OUTDOOR FLUORESCENT FIXTURES MOUNTED INSIDE TO CREATE A LIGHT BOX / SIGN

LETTERS CUT FROM 1/4" PLEXIGLAS (COLOR OF YOUR CHOICE)

CORRUGATED STEEL FACING (WRAPS SIDE)

ARTIFICIAL FOLIAGE

BRICK VENEER OVER BASE

Happy Holidays

NO ROOM AT THE INN

② FRONT ELEVATION
3/4" =1'

③ SIDE ELEVATION
3/4" =1'

① PLAN VIEW
3/4" =1'

GENERAL NOTES

PROJECT:
NO ROOM AT THE INN LIGHTING EXTRAVAGANZA

SCALE:
3/4" = 1'

1. ALL CONSTRUCTION TO BE 3/4" PLYWOOD, EXCEPT WHERE NOTED

2. INSTALL AN OUTDOOR-LIGHTING SURGE SUPPRESSOR

3. DO NOT ALLOW BARE BULBS TO TOUCH ANY PART OF THE WOODEN STRUCTURE

4. CUT ACCESS PANELS ON BACK OF SIGN, HINGE VENTILATE, AND WEATHERPROOF AS REQUIRED

5. IF YOU DON'T KNOW WHAT YOU'RE DOIN', GO SIT ON THE BENCH, BEFORE YOU BURN THE HOUSE DOWN!

6. PAINT TO SUIT—BUT HAVE YOUR WIFE PICK OUT THE COLORS, YOU HAVE CRAP FOR TASTE

JUNK FOR JOY!

✳ ✳ ✳

The holidays are always busy and you need every timesaving tip you can get! Here's a way to decorate your home and feed your guests with tasty treats all at the same time! Most of these ingredients come straight out of a bag, so there's little or no cooking involved! These kitschy decorations will fill your house with the joy of junk food and send that diet packing.

The gorgeous wall wreath is made of delectable snack cakes, the Little Town of Bethle-Ham and Cheese of tiny sandwiches and crackers. It would take a village idiot to pass up these treats. And, if you're looking to transform your buffet into a winter wonderland, the marshmallow snowman is the fellow for you. A bag of green chips and some cherry tomatoes transform an old gelatin ring mold into a lovely tabletop wreath the whole family will enjoy. At the center of it all, we present our featured project, a stunning donut tree.

YOU WILL NEED

One 34-ounce coffee can
Plaster of paris
⅜-inch wooden dowel rods cut to the
  following measures:
   * One 28 inch
   * Four 9 inch
   * Four 8 inch
   * Four 7 inch
   * Four 6 inch
   * Four 5 inch
   * Four 4 inch
Six 12-inch strips masking tape
6 round wooden joint wheels (from a
  Tinker Toy set)
Round rat-tail file (optional)
Wood glue
1 container green food-safe paint
⅜-inch flat craft paintbrush
Hot-glue gun and glue sticks

1 It is best to prepare your tree forms at least an hour or two in advance, so the plaster of paris is dry enough to hold the dowel rod firmly (it will be fully dry in 24 hours). Fill the coffee can three-fourths full of plaster of paris, mixed according to the package directions.

2 Place the 28-inch dowel in the center of the can with the liquid plaster. Using the precut masking tape strips, make a series of stabilizing straps across the rim of the can. Double-check to make sure it is plumb before allowing it to set. Let dry completely. This is the trunk of the tree.

3 Slide the round wooden joint wheels onto the center trunk of the tree, spacing them evenly. They should be snug but not tight. If they are, do not force them. Remove them and widen the hole with a round rat-tail file, being careful not to make the hole too large.

4 Begin to place the dowel rod branches into the holes of the joint wheels, starting with the 9-inch dowels in the lowest wheel and working up the

Assorted felt, ribbon, and bric-a-brac
71 doughnuts in assorted sizes

wheels in order of diminishing size, ending with the 4-inch dowels; secure with a small amount of wood glue. Stagger the placement of the branches to give the tree a full look. If you suspect any wheels are too loose, use a little wood glue to ensure stability.

5 Allow all glue to dry completely.

6 Paint the tree structure with the green paint using the craft brush. Let dry.

7 Using the hot-glue gun and sticks, decorate the coffee can with felt, ribbon, and bric-a-brac.

8 When you are ready to "serve," take one doughnut and pierce it on top of the tree.

9 Now fill those branches with delicious doughnuts, your guests are starving!

✳ Put that obsessive-compulsive disorder to good use this Kitschmas by creating this fabulous marshmallow snowman. Start with a styrofoam base, cover it with plastic wrap, and start sticking mini marshmallows on the form using tons of toothpicks.

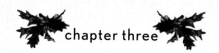
Bring the Kitsch Out of the Kitchen, *It's Time to Eat!*

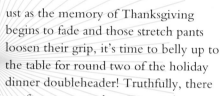

Just as the memory of Thanksgiving begins to fade and those stretch pants loosen their grip, it's time to belly up to the table for round two of the holiday dinner doubleheader! Truthfully, there is very little to distinguish these two evil-twin feasts from one another. We eat the same thing, sit in the same seats, and fall into the same family roles. It's time to put the fun back into the dysfunctional family holiday dinner.

Let's just leave Thanksgiving as is, shall we? Without that big fancy turkey dinner, it's just a bunch of parades and a couple of football games. Kitschmas, on the other hand, offers a world of imaginative possibilities to be explored. In the following pages, you'll find a few food-for-thought menu ideas for full meals, but they need not be limited to the big family dinner (or, in the case of Tiny Tim, a teensy, individual feast). This light-hearted approach can be applied to all sorts of holiday eating opportunities.

Start with a specific meal genre. Let's say brunch. Really, say it. Say the word "brunch" a thousand or so times with any other words that come to mind. . . . Let's also imagine that you happen to be a television rerun savant. You might come up with a "Kitschmas Brady Brunch!" Imagine the menu! Marsha Potatoes, Jancakes, Greggs and Ham! Alice Calm, Alice Bright Eggnogg! Okay, so their holiday special wasn't that great, but the brunch could be fabulous!

YES YOU CAN,
it's Kitschmas!

✳ ✳ ✳

Plug in the can opener, it's time to cook! If you just can't let go of your traditional holiday menu but you like the idea of a kitschy challenge, put a new spin on this year's feast with the Yes You Can, It's Kitschmas! Dinner. This menu will grace your table with all the usual suspects, but since all the recipes are made from canned goods, it will add that certain Kitschmas kick.

A nearby aluminum tree, delightfully trimmed with tin cans and lights, will be a magnificent accent to your thoroughly modern masterpiece. Most of these recipes are very well known or are listed on the can itself (i.e., the infamous green bean casserole, made with canned soup, canned beans, and canned fried onions); we have detailed recipes only for the more obscure dishes. This is the easiest holiday dinner you will ever prepare. Think you can't do it? Yes you can!

Menu

- Kitschy Cola Canned Ham, Ya Ya (page 60)
- Can-Do Caramelized Potatoes (page 61)
- Canned green bean casserole
- Canned cranberry sauce (leave in the shape of the can!)
- Canned yams with marshmallows
- Canned fruit cocktail

KITSCHY COLA CANNED HAM, ya ya

* * *

Okay, so it's not really a Creole recipe, but the name is catchy and the recipe did come from a friend in Louisiana, so like the song sort of says, "kitschy kitschy ya ya da da!" Cooking never sounded so fun and easy! Forget those complicated magazine ham recipes that take hours to prepare. This recipe is tasty and will give you plenty of time to pop open a can of beer and relax before dinner.

YOU WILL NEED

12 ounces of your favorite cola
2 tablespoons brown mustard
1 tablespoon Worcestershire sauce
1 garlic clove, minced
One 5-pound canned ham
1 cup dark brown sugar
One 20-ounce can pineapple slices
Maraschino cherries (enough to make it pretty)

Serves VI to VIII

1 Preheat the oven to 325 degrees F.

2 Combine the cola, mustard, Worcestershire sauce, and garlic in a bowl.

3 Place the ham in a roasting pan and score the top in a crisscross pattern using a big, sharp knife.

4 Pat the brown sugar onto the top of the ham, and slowly pour the cola mixture over it.

5 Slap on the pineapple (as many as you can fit on top) and use toothpicks to stick a cherry in the center of each.

6 Bake for 1 hour, basting every 10 to 15 minutes.

CAN-DO CARAMELIZED POTATOES

* * *

Canned potatoes aren't just for camping and fallout shelters anymore; we say they are fit for the most highfalutin of holiday festivities. You'll feel like an uptown culinary sophisticate when you serve this little side dish.

YOU WILL NEED

Three 15-ounce cans whole white
　potatoes
¾ cup butter
¾ cup light brown sugar
Fresh rosemary to taste

Serves VI to VIII

1 Drain the potatoes completely.

2 Melt the butter in a skillet. Add the brown sugar and cook until the sugar is dissolved and the mixture is bubbly.

3 Add the potatoes and cook, stirring, until heated through, about 5 minutes.

4 Garnish with the rosemary (told ya it was easy).

TINY TIM'S
teensy feast

✳ ✳ ✳

There is something enchanting about Kitschmas that turns us all into wide-eyed suckers for adorably cute miniature tchotchkes. From elfin tree ornaments, tabletop villages, and blizzards in a snow globe to the incredible shrunken world of toys, it seems that anything can be made charming if small enough.

It is in this spirit that we present a magical mini-meal alternative to an area of the holidays that never seems to get smaller: the traditional binge banquet. It's a clever way to sneak portion control into your family feast. As if sprinkled with pixie dust, this tiny turkey (really a Rock Cornish game hen) is served on a wee bed of dressing and garnished with pearl onions, miniature corn cobs, champagne grapes, and baby lettuce. It's a small world, after all.

Menu

- Tiny Tim's Turkey (page 64)
- Your favorite dressing
- Pearl onions
- Canned baby corn
- Champagne grapes
- Baby lettuce salad

TINY TIM'S TURKEY

✳ ✳ ✳

The weird thing about Rock Cornish game hens is that they really do look like someone stuck a big tom turkey into a copier and pushed the reduce button. The result is almost hallucinogenic, like a holiday dinner in Alice's Wonderland. Have fun with it; if you really want to push the distortion of proportion, serve it on toy china, seating everyone at small tables and chairs usually reserved for the kids.

The following recipe is written per individual serving, since each guest gets to single-handedly devour their own bird. You will need to multiply each ingredient quantity by the total number of guests that you plan to serve. Bon appétit! And we do mean petite!

YOU WILL NEED

½ cup melted butter
½ cup chopped onion
¼ cup finely chopped celery
¼ cup finely chopped bell pepper
Half a 4½-ounce can of mushrooms,
   drained and chopped
2 cloves garlic, minced
2 teaspoons dried basil
1 teaspoon dried oregano
2 teaspoons chopped fresh parsley
Salt and pepper to taste
1 Rock Cornish game hen, sans gizzards
   and guts

Serves I

1 Preheat the oven to 325 degrees F.

2 In a mixing bowl, combine ¼ cup of the butter, the onion, celery, bell pepper, mushrooms, garlic, basil, oregano, parsley, and salt and pepper.

3 Season the hen with salt and pepper inside and out. Stuff with the vegetable-herb mixture.

4 Place in a baking dish, breast-side up, with legs tied as you would a large turkey.

5 Baste with the remaining ¼ cup melted butter.

6 Cover and bake for 60 to 90 minutes.

7 Remove the cover, set the oven to broil, and broil the hen for a few minutes to brown the skin, watching closely to prevent burning.

HOLLY GOLIGHTLY'S
breakfast at Tiffany's

✳ ✳ ✳

The beloved character of Holly Golightly has inspired countless fashion plates through the years; why not let her inspire the plates for your morning-after Champagne breakfast. In the sanitized film version, Audrey Hepburn's stylish presence, dripping in Givenchy, transformed the book's "hooker with a heart of gold" into a capricious party girl. This fashion icon's beauty could actually inspire men to lavish her with gifts and money, simply to be in her luminous presence. Nothing dirty was going on in the movie; it was all about fun, fashion, and innuendo!

So gather your stray-cat friends who didn't go home for the holidays because they blew their paycheck on a new pair of Prada pumps. Tell everyone the theme and suggest that they dress to impress. The menu is simple and no cooking is involved. Who knows if the stove pilot is even lit? Quel drag! The only preparation is a fabulous "diamond"-encrusted Champagne bucket trimmed with silver-painted holly as the spotlight centerpiece.

Menu

- Bear claws in bags

- Milk in a martini glass (it's for the cat)

- Single Girl's Champagne Bucket (page 67)

- Champagne

- Ice

SINGLE GIRL'S CHAMPAGNE BUCKET

✳ ✳ ✳

Since Breakfast at Tiffany's is the defining moment of urban chic and "the little black dress," this centerpiece is a monochromatic study in black, white, and the silvery shades in between. This breakfast is all about the Champagne, so get plenty to go around—the guests on this list eat like birds and drink like fish! Besides, if you want to look like Audrey, you'd better back away from the gravy. Create this sparkling centerpiece to distract your guests from their hunger.

YOU WILL NEED

1 galvanized tin bucket, 6½ inches wide and 6 inches high
Masking tape (optional)
Hot-glue gun and glue sticks
About two hundred fifty 12-mm faceted acrylic craft gemstones
Plastic holly sprays (enough to create an arrangement around the base of the bucket)
1 can of gray spray primer
1 can of good-quality silver spray paint
Silver spray glitter
One 18-inch pearl trailer (a wedding-supply item of delicate pearls strung loosely on a series of monofilament threads)
Fine floral wire
Champagne bucket
A pair of oversized dark sunglasses

1   If your silver bucket is like the one used for this demonstration, you will have a raised ridge that runs around the bucket about 2 inches from the top, creating a logical boundary to fill with gemstones. If your bucket does not have this feature, you can define your own band using masking tape.

2   Using hot glue, begin filling the top band area with closely set gemstones, until it has the rich look of pavé diamonds.

3   Take your collection of holly leaves and spray them with a light coating of primer, being careful to get all sides. Let dry completely.

4   Spray the holly bright silver with the silver paint. Let dry completely.

5   Add a little extra shimmer with a few layers of silver spray glitter, letting each layer dry between applications.

6   Take the pearl trailer and wrap it around the base of the bucket, attaching the ends together with the fine floral wire.

7   Begin arranging the holly sprays into the pearl trailer, tucking and tangling the holly within the monofilament threads.

8   Place a bottle of Champagne into the bucket, add ice, hang a stylish set of oversized dark sunglasses from the rim, and put on some Henry Mancini music. It's time to drink our Kitschmas dinner!

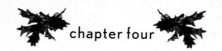

chapter four

Figgy Pudding
and Other Desserts of Kitschmas Past

T he flashy finale to any great meal is a decadent dessert. Throughout time, people have marked the season by splurging on the finest and richest desserts of the year. If you yearn for nostalgia and feel more grounded by holiday tradition, we suggest that you take a look at the sweet treats from those "good old days." Now take a second look. When it comes to food, you'll see that old is not always best. Adventurous cooks will find these recipes fascinating, but they may send many modern palates running for cover. For fun in any case, let's take a look back at what made mouths water in Kitschmases past, to see how things have changed over the years.

These epicurean epilogues are a great way to celebrate the season while saluting the past. From fruitcakes and figgy pudding to the mystery of mince meat, these "double dog dare ya" recipes will fill ye olde yuletide festivities with the flavor of yore and burn a memorable impression that will last for eons to come.

◁ Here's a fun twist on the traditional fruitcake for those high-maintenance vegetarians who ruin your holiday dinner by picking at their food and insisting to know each ingredient of every dish.

WHAT A BUNCH OF
fruitcakes!

✳ ✳ ✳

This is the kitschiest of all holiday cakes. Who hasn't eagerly opened a beautifully wrapped present only to find a heavy, dark brown cake (of questionable vintage) covered in shiny red and green gelatinous fruit shards? Does anyone really love these cakes? Rumor has it that many a mail-order fruitcake is used as a festive doorstop at holiday open houses. However, we seem to be stuck with them; this tradition goes back to the ancient Roman era. It's time to acknowledge the kitsch factor of fruitcakes and really have some fun with it.

Since it is doubtful that anyone really eats these things, start with a generic recipe (like the one following, or your great-aunt's favorite) and focus on the packaging—that's where the passive-aggressive fun begins. There must be someone on your gift list that falls into the "fruitcake" category, whether they are freaky, off kilter, or a little light in their loafers. SOMEONE you know probably fits one of these descriptions (if not, you may be the one). Let's don't go overboard and cause the ruin of someone's holiday. Use a light hand, a funny card, and only send fruitcakes to candidates with a good sense of humor (i.e., don't send The Certifiable, page 75, to your fragile cousin in the state sanitarium). Be nice, it's Kitschmas!

⬧ Include a fun card that says, "You so crazy!"

YOUR BASIC FRUITCAKE

✳ ✳ ✳

YOU WILL NEED

2½ cups all-purpose flour

1 teaspoon baking soda

2 eggs, lightly beaten

One 28-ounce jar mincemeat

One 14-ounce can sweetened
  condensed milk

2 cups chopped mixed glacé (candied)
  fruit (available in well-stocked markets,
  especially at Kitschmastime)

1 cup chopped walnuts

Whole glacé (candied) cherries and
  pecan halves for garnish

Serves VI to VIII (theoretically)

1 Preheat the oven to 300 degrees F.

2 Grease two 9-by-5-inch loaf pans.

3 In a bowl, sift together the flour and baking soda; set aside.

4 In a large bowl, combine the eggs, mincemeat, condensed milk, mixed fruit, and walnuts. Add the dry ingredients and mix well.

5 Divide the batter evenly between the prepared pans. Bake for 1 hour and 20 minutes, or until a toothpick inserted into the center comes out clean.

6 Let cool 15 minutes before turning out the cakes onto wire racks; let cool completely.

7 Garnish with the glacé cherries and pecan halves (make it pretty).

**Add extra nuts to this recipe to really
drive the point home for the holidays.**

＊ ＊ ＊

PAGE 68 **The Vegetarian Fruitcake**

Search the Internet for a wacky vegan fruitcake recipe. Add a bunch of wheat grass to the mix to ensure that it's completely inedible. Hope they get the message and never come to your house for dinner again. Pack it up in recycled materials, raffia, or hay, and tie it with a nice macramé belt. Peace, man.

PAGE 71 **The Certifiable Fruitcake**

A quilted coat lining forms this beautiful padded-cell box. Restrain your cake with a heavy-duty canvas straightjacket, and make sure to cut a small window in the lid for proper ventilation and a little sunshine. Tie it all up with a series of sturdy nylon straps.

PAGE 78 **The Paranoid Fruitcake**

Cover the box with creepy doll eyes and include a nice card with a tender message like, "We all got together and decided this would be the perfect gift. Signed, Anonymous."

◁ **Send the Closet Fruitcake to those "Don't ask, don't tell" names on your holiday list.**

✳ ✳ ✳

PAGE 74 **The Closet Fruitcake**

Perfect for that hard-to-shop-for bachelor uncle! Build a sturdy wooden box with a top that looks like a closet door. Glue, nail, or wire it shut— whatever you have to do to keep that thing closed. It doesn't matter what you do with the cake; if you build the box correctly, no one will ever get the door open.

OPPOSITE **That Toothless Cousin Fruitcake**

The one who always wanted to date you! Just turn the loaf pan upside down, add a few kitschy details and some old toy truck parts, and you are ready to roll! To make it extra trashy, alternately thicken and thin cake batter with mayonnaise and beer.

There's no place like home for the holidays, no matter how far away you roll!

HERE'S YOUR FRIGGING
pudding

* * *

All right, already! Here's your frigging pudding! Jeez! It's like a scene from Kitschmas Village of the Damned. One can only imagine a surly gang of zombielike carolers chanting and scratching at the door, demanding to be fed, or else! What about this dessert would inspire such desperation? The answer is crystal clear: this Victorian-era holiday recipe has suet in it! Of course it does. These caroling fiends need kidney fat to survive. Can things get more frightening? Try this recipe IF YOU DARE. One thing is certain: if you give the ravenous carolers what they crave, they may never darken your door again. We wish you a scary Kitschmas and a creepy New Year!

YOU WILL NEED

¾ cup all-purpose flour
Pinch of salt
1 cup dried unseasoned fine bread crumbs
½ cup dark brown sugar
1 teaspoon baking powder
1 teaspoon ground allspice
1½ cups chopped dried figs
Finely grated zest and juice of 1 lemon
2 tablespoons milk
2 eggs, lightly beaten
¼ pound suet (the solid, dense fat that encloses beef or sheep kidneys; ask your butcher), shredded
5 gummy orange candies
1 tablespoon chopped dried fig

1 Sift the flour and salt together into a large bowl.

2 Add the bread crumbs, brown sugar, baking powder, and allspice and stir to combine.

3 Add the figs, lemon zest and juice, milk, and eggs and beat together. The mixture should have a soft, dropping consistency. Fold in the suet.

4 Spoon into a greased 1-quart pudding mold and cover securely.

5 Steam until it has a very moist, cake consistency, about 3 hours.

6 Garnish with the gummy orange candy slices topped with the chopped dried fig.

Serves VI to VIII zombie carolers

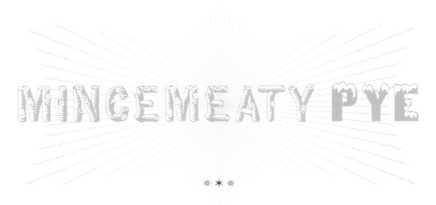

MINCEMEATY PYE

* * *

For centuries people have gathered around a steaming pot, taking turns stirring their precious mincemeat filling in a clockwise direction and making their holiday wishes. Mincemeat pie (a.k.a. Christmas pye) is one of the most traditional of all holiday desserts. However, the recipe has evolved over the years into a big, huge pants-on-fire lie, leaving us to wonder, "Where's the beef?" Today's commercial mincemeat pie fillings are pasteurized impostors of their gutsier ancestors. Fabled to have once included such exotic ingredients as ox tongue, mutton, veal, or venison, it seems that whatever fell in the pot would do, which was then sweetened with fruits (fresh, candied, dried, and otherwise).

Here's your chance to find out what real mincemeat is all about and to live out those Dickensian dreams of Christmases long, long ago. Our recipe spares you the exotic meats, using only standard-issue stew beef. You don't want to scare the stuffing out of your guests after a big holiday meal by telling them that your pie is packed with ox tongue.

So, what was it about those pie recipes that made them so loved they were carefully handed down from generation to generation? Get down with your medieval self, cook up a big sweet meaty pye, and find out for once and for all.

YOU WILL NEED

1 pound lean beef stew meat

3 pounds Granny Smith apples, cored and chopped

⅓ pound coarsely ground beef suet (the solid dense fat that encloses beef or sheep kidneys; ask your butcher)

1 cup dark brown sugar

½ cup white vinegar

½ cup apple juice

1 Place the stew meat in a 4-quart pot with water to cover. Bring to a boil, reduce the heat, cover, and simmer until tender, 45 minutes to 1 hour. Drain and process in a food processor until coarsely chopped. Return to the pot.

2 Preheat the oven to 375 degrees F.

3 Add all the remaining ingredients to the pot. Bring to a simmer, stirring often. Reduce the heat to a slow simmer, cover, and cook for 1 hour, stirring occasionally. Remove from the heat and let cool completely.

4 Prepare the pie crusts and line two 9-inch pie dishes.

¼ cup rum
¼ cup molasses
2½ cups raisins
1½ cups dried currants
1 teaspoon ground cloves
½ teaspoon freshly grated nutmeg
½ teaspoon ground allspice
1 teaspoon ground cinnamon
Two 9-inch double pie crusts (your
   favorite recipe)

Makes two IX-inch pies

🌜 Place half of the meat mixture into one pie shell. Cover with a top crust and seal the edges. Cut a few slits in the top for ventilation. Repeat with the remaining meat mixture, pie shell, and top crust.

🌜 Bake for 1 hour, or until golden brown and bubbly. Serve warm.

NOTE
For all of you on those controversial carnivore diets, the only zone this recipe falls into is the twilight zone.

GEE WHIZ GELATIN

✳ ✳ ✳

Gelamold mania rocketed to popularity during the mid-twentieth century like an atomic bomb. As earthlings raced to space, so did our food. With TV dinners, freeze-dried coffee, and fortified fruit-flavored cereals, science was creating safer, happier food products that looked more like test-tube miracles than anything organic. Gone was the savagery of meat pies and suet puddings; it was time to leave the cave and face the brave new world ahead.

Gelatin inspired an explosion of creativity from kitchen-bound housewives everywhere who secretly aspired to be sculptors, chemists, or world-renowned chefs. It became an artistic medium to be mastered, and the results were what Kitschmas legends are made of. The jiggly, jolly dessert could and can take on any flavor, color, or even, with the clever use of molds, shape. No holiday was complete without a perfectly formed gelatin jewel to wiggle and wow the crowd.

This quivering blast-from-the-past dessert has been created in the spirit of the space craze and its promise of a better tomorrow through the advances of science. Green and red cherries float like planets orbiting the sun. It is topped by an atomic-style tree made of craft straws and gum drops. With flashing twinkle lights under a glass plate, this stunning dessert glows like radioactive space goo.

Duck and cover! It's Kitschmas!

YOU WILL NEED

Three 3-ounce boxes sparkling white grape–flavored gelatin
1 cup boiling water
3 cups ginger ale (Champagne or club soda can be substituted)
1 cup drained red and green maraschino cherries
One 11-inch glass serving dish
Pencil
One 8½-inch bamboo skewer
1 aerosol can cap

1 Lightly grease a 6-cup gelatin ring mold.

2 In a bowl, mix the gelatin with the boiling water and stir until dissolved, about 2 minutes. Refrigerate for 10 minutes.

3 Stir in the ginger ale; the mixture will be foamy. Refrigerate for 20 minutes.

4 Stir in the 1 cup of red and green cherries. Transfer the mixture to the prepared mold. Cover with plastic wrap and chill until set, at least 6 hours or up to overnight.

Floral foam or Styrofoam (enough to fill
    the aerosol cap)
Ice pick
Three 9-inch green plastic craft straws
    (green translucent drinking straws
    will do)
Scissors
Floral wire
Wire cutters
1 strong, thick needle
19 gumdrops
One 9½-by-3-inch springform baking
    pan
1 flashing multicolored light string
Toothpicks
23 colorful gummy candies for garnish

Serves IX

✳ ✳ ✳

5 To unmold, run a small sharp paring knife around the sides of the mold. Place the mold upright in a shallow bowl filled with enough warm (not hot) water to come halfway up the sides of the mold for 30 seconds. Wet the glass serving plate slightly, invert the mold onto it, and refrigerate until ready to serve.

6 Using the pencil, measuring from the blunt end, mark the bamboo skewer at the 3½-, 5-, and 6½-inch marks.

7 To make the tree stand, push the aerosol cap into the floral foam to fill the cap tightly. Trim the excess with a knife.

8 To make the trunk, punch a small hole in the center of the top of the cap with an ice pick or metal skewer and insert the bamboo skewer through the hole and into the foam, keeping it as straight as possible. Slide 1 craft straw over the bamboo skewer and make a pencil mark on the straw ½ inch below the top of the skewer. Remove the straw, trim at the mark, and replace over the bamboo skewer.

9 Cut floral wire to the following lengths: three pieces at 4 inches, three pieces at 3 inches, and three pieces at 2 inches. Keeping the straw in place, locate the pencil marks on the bamboo skewer. At these marks, create three tiers of branches with the wires by piercing the straw at the placement point of each wire with the strong needle. Thread the wires through the prepierced holes in like-sized sets of three, starting with the longest wires at the lowest mark. Each layer of branches should look like a wire asterisk.

✳ ✳ ✳

10 Cut the remaining craft straws into the following lengths: six pieces at 1½ inches, six pieces at ⅞ inch, six pieces at ½ inch. Slide the straw pieces over the wire branches.

11 Gently push 1 gumdrop onto each branch of the tree, and one on the top of the skewer. Set aside.

12 Place the springform pan where you plan to display your finished dessert, keeping in mind the location of a wall outlet or extension cord.

13 Place the entire light string in the pan, arranging the lights in a very random, tangled mess.

14 Holding the pan upright, open the spring mechanism all the way to release the bottom of the pan. Sneak the plug out the side of the bottom, pull through as much length of cord as you need to reach the outlet, and snap the bottom back in place.

15 When ready to serve, plug in the lights, remove the plated gelatin ring from the refrigerator, and snuggle it on top of the pan of flashing lights. Carefully center the gumdrop tree in the middle of the gelatin ring.

16 Finally, garnish the gelatin with a satellite-like halo of gummy candies on toothpicks to give it a little extra space-age spirit. Gee whiz, that looks swell! Serve chilled.

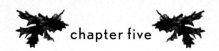
Get into the Kitschmas Spirits!

From the time we first started putting tiny umbrellas in mai tais, the presentation of a cocktail has become as splashy as a cheesy lounge act. With this in mind, imagine the Kitschmas possibilities! These festive recipes have been created to go hand in hand with their presentation. The glass, the garnish, even the swizzle stick can really add to the overall pizzazz of the libation. Many of these drinks are stiff and strong, to say the least. There is a reason for this: these are "event drinks," and should keep you buzzin' all the way, on that one-horse open sleigh. This chapter is for booze hounds who prefer their holidays on ice, with a twist.

In our culture, we have more words for getting loaded than Eskimos have for snow. Here are just a few: blind, blitzed, blotto, bombed, boozed up, buzzed, crocked, drunk, hammered, high, juiced, legless, lit, looped, loose, pickled, plastered, plowed, sloppy, sloshed, soaked, soused, stewed, stoned, tanked, tight, tipsy, toasted, totaled, trashed, wasted, zonked, or just plain schnockered.

◁ 'Tis the season to get tipsy! Enjoy a Frosty the Chocoholic Snowman (left, page 91), Chocolate Candy Cone (center, page 90), Santa's Little Helper (right, page 90).

....AND A PARTRIDGE
in a pear tree

✳ ✳ ✳

Come on, get happy! This pop-culture Kitschmas cocktail has a fresh-pear-and-citrus flavor that will definitely put you on the road to happiness. Gee whiz, it's got the fabulous "limon" taste of Sprite in it! What could be more swell? It's refreshing, bubbly, and perfect for a trip down memory lane, in a big painted bus.

YOU WILL NEED

1 frosted glass tumbler large enough to hold a small pear
1 roll of electrical tape in primary colors (red, yellow, blue, and black; available at hardware stores)
X-Acto knife or scissors
A few sheets of craft foam (available at craft stores) in fun colors
1 long swizzle stick
Hot-glue gun and glue stick
Spray adhesive or glue stick
Photos of the Partridge Family (search the Internet), printed to fit key tags
1 metal-rimmed paper key tag (available at office-supply stores)
1 small frozen pear
Crushed ice
1½ ounces pear brandy
½ ounce Rose's Lime Juice
¼ ounce Limoncello (sweet lemon liqueur)
1 can of Sprite

Serves I

1 Start with the decoration of the tumbler, as a salute to the Partridge Family bus: create your own Mondrian-esque design using the colored electrical tape.

2 Using the X-Acto knife, cut a leaf or tree design out of the foam sheets. (The design should be reminiscent of the groovy graphics that preceded each fabulous episode.) Hot-glue the swizzle stick to the foam cutout. Cut another leaf and hot-glue it over the previously joined area to finish and hide any glue.

3 Using a quick burst of spray adhesive to the back of the photo, paste a photo of your favorite Partridge* onto the key tag, and hang it from the foam leaf or tree.

4 Place the frozen pear in the glass.

5 Add crushed ice to your taste, the pear brandy, lime juice, and Limoncello.

6 Fill the balance with Sprite.

*You might make a couple extra copies of David Cassidy. There are middle-aged women everywhere who have never let go of their *Teen Beat* fantasies of Keith Partridge.

SANTA'S
little helper

✳ ✳ ✳

'This little hot shot tastes like a glass of warm milk and gingerbread cookies. Leave this out for Santa and he'll be feeling no pain—your stocking might just get a little extra stuffing (a little last-minute bribery never hurt anybody).

YOU WILL NEED

One 2-ounce shot glass shaped like a
  miniature old-fashioned glass
1 saucer
Miniature cookies
1 tablespoon hot milk
½ ounce Bailey's Irish Cream liqueur
½ ounce Goldschläger
½ ounce butterscotch schnapps

Serves I

1 Place your little glass in the middle of the saucer. The charm in this presentation is the diminutive scale. Everything looks as if it was made for an elf.

2 With a paring knife, carefully cut a slot in 1 miniature cookie and place it on the rim, like a lemon wedge.

3 Arrange more cookies around the glass.

4 Pour the hot milk into the shot glass.

5 Add the remaining ingredients.

6 Set it out for Santa with a list of really expensive gift ideas. You never know.

Chocolate Candy Cane

For a peppy pick-me-up to get the party started, mix one part grenadine, one part peppermint vodka, and one part white Godiva liqueur in a tall shot glass. Garnish with a candy cane dipped in melted chocolate. These minty devils are both decorative and intoxicating. . . your guests will love 'em!

FROSTY
the chocoholic snowman

* * *

Clearly, this is the secret behind Frosty's jolly, happy soul. This sneaky martini has a surprisingly smooth chocolate flavor that gives you no warning before it knocks you on your fanny. Don't be fooled by its creamy sweetness—this sucker packs a secondary punch that'll have you running through the snow in your Skivvies like a drunken snowman.

YOU WILL NEED

1 Z-stem martini glass
1 white lollipop stick (available at craft and baking stores)
3 mini marshmallows
One 3-inch piece of white pipe cleaner
Hot-glue gun and glue sticks
1 miniature liquor bottle (I found these little liquor bottles in the dollhouse section of a craft store. I guess dolls have drinking issues just like the rest of us.)
1 chocolate chip
A few chocolate sprinkles
Sugar to rim glass
1 ounce vodka
1 ounce white crème de cacao
1 ounce Bailey's Irish Cream liqueur
Splash or two of heavy cream
Ice

Serves 1

1 Put the martini glass in the freezer to chill.

2 Use the lollipop stick to pierce through 2 of the mini marshmallows. Angle each one differently to make Frosty look loose and looped.

3 Make little arms for the snowman by twisting the pipe cleaner around the lollipop stick above the marshmallows.

4 Hot-glue the tiny liquor bottle to one of the hands.

5 Skewer the third marshmallow (the head) at a drunken angle above the arms.

6 Wet the top of the snowman's head and place the chocolate chip on top as a cheerful hat.

7 Wet the "face" of the top marshmallow and use the chocolate sprinkles to make the eyes, nose, and mouth.

8 Place some sugar on a plate. Remove the glass from the freezer, moisten the rim, and dip into the sugar.

9 Mix the vodka, crème de cacao, Bailey's, and cream over ice in a shaker full of ice.

10 Strain into the martini glass. Rest ye merry swizzle snowman in the glass.

the
SUGARPLUM FAIRY

* * *

After a few of these concoctions, Tchaikovsky's *Nutcracker* story starts making a lot more sense. He and author E. T. A. Hoffmann must have tossed back quite a few vodka cocktails before imagining toys coming to life and giant rats with swords. This girly potent potable is a dream in pink much like Clara's hallucinogenic vision of sugarplums dancing in her head. The swizzle stick is topped by a plastic ballerina cake topper and the glass even gets a tutu. Hand this fancy-pants drink to a big, burly guy and watch him squirm like you just handed him a purse.

YOU WILL NEED

1 tall collins glass

Hot-glue gun and glue sticks

1 small ballerina cake topper

1 pink swizzle stick

1 pink straw

2 ounces citrus vodka

½ ounce Cointreau

1 ounce lemon juice

Splash of cranberry juice

Ice

2 teaspoons sugar, plus extra for rimming
   the glass

One 4-by-24-inch strip of pink tulle

1 clear rubber band (available anywhere
   they sell hair bands and barrettes)

Scissors

Serves 1

1 Put the collins glass in the freezer to chill.

2 Hot-glue the ballerina cake topper to the end of the swizzle stick.

3 Slide the swizzle stick into the straw; set aside.

4 In a blender, combine the vodka, Cointreau, and lemon and cranberry juices with ice and the two teaspoons sugar. Blend into a pink icy slush.

5 Place some sugar on a plate. Remove the glass from the freezer, moisten the rim, and dip in the sugar. (Colored sugar makes it extra fancy.)

6 With the strip of pink tulle, make a quick tutu for the glass by just gathering it around the glass and slipping the rubber band around its "waist." Trim with scissors to the desired shape.

7 Pour this frosty pink dream into the collins glass and add the ballerina straw/swizzle stick. Voilà!

SANTA'S HOT
buttered rum balls

✳ ✳ ✳

What's Christmas without rum balls? (See page 29 for more on Kitschmas balls.) This hot drink is loaded with suggestive possibilities, so serve it last. Everyone will be a lot looser at the end of the evening as the winter chill sets in.

YOU WILL NEED
1 teaspoon powdered sugar
1 glass Irish coffee cup
½ cup boiling water
¼ cup dark rum
1 teaspoon butter
Pinch of freshly ground nutmeg
2 marshmallows
1 cinnamon stick

Serves I

1 Place the powdered sugar in the Irish coffee cup.

2 Add the boiling water, rum, and butter. Stir until the butter is melted.

3 Sprinkle with nutmeg.

4 Drop in the marshmallows, dunking them with a cinnamon stick to wet and soften them.

5 They should be sticky now, so, using your best judgment, place the cinnamon stick wherever you like.

OFFICE KITSCHMAS
party punch

✳ ✳ ✳

A collection of celebratory kitschy beverages would not be complete without a salute to the yearly humiliation of office parties, where everyone drinks too much, says too much, and may end up wearing too little. Raise a glass of this office party punch to the spectacle of Helen from Accounting "gettin' jiggy with it" on the dance floor with Bob from human resources. The fun part about this concoction, besides being very tasty, is the schnockered schecretary decoration. As the drinks go down and the hours slip away, she'll lose her balance and slip into the abyss of the punch bowl, lamp shade and all.

YOU WILL NEED

For the schnockered secretary ice block
1 fashion doll dressed as a secretary
1 small plastic cup
Hot-glue gun and glue sticks
Beaded fringe
Thin floral wire
A few doll-sized office props (calculator, briefcase, etc.)
1 mini dollhouse-sized string of holiday lights
One 16-ounce plastic drinking cup
Cranberry juice
A few thin orange slices
Masking tape

1 This is going to be fun. Start this project a few days before the party and leave the schnockered secretary ice block in the freezer until ready to serve. Take one of your daughter's battered fashion dolls and dress her up as if she is in the midst of a career-ending, desktop striptease. (I added a little padding around the middle and the hips to make her look like she has been stuck behind a desk all year.)

2 Craft a mini lamp shade using the small plastic cup; hot-glue the beaded fringe around the rim. Let dry, then hot-glue the lamp shade to the doll as shown.

3 Hot-glue and/or use the floral wire to attach the office props, including the mini light string, in position on the doll to complete the picture. Here I have used a briefcase, a calculator, a string of Christmas lights, and a gold pipe cleaner, all found in the dollhouse accessory department of a craft store. Use your imagination (or base it on actual events from a past party).

4 Place her in the 16-ounce plastic cup and fill with three parts cranberry juice, one part water, and the orange slices. Prop her up vertically in the cup with a series of cleverly placed strips of masking tape across the rim of the cup. Stick her in the freezer for a day or so.

For the punch
5 cups chilled cranberry juice
2½ cups chilled orange juice
2½ cups vodka (3½ cups if you really
    want things to get wild, less if you are
    making it for family)
2 ounces Cointreau
¾ teaspoon ground cinnamon
½ teaspoon allspice
¼ teaspoon freshly ground nutmeg
2 oranges, thinly sliced

Serves XV to XX

✳ ✳ ✳

5 Remove tape and unmold the secretarial sculpture from the plastic container by running the outside of the cup under warm water to loosen.

6 Place her in the center of a punch bowl. Add about an inch of water and ice cubes to the bowl and stick everything back in the freezer for a few hours. This will give the base a bit more stability.

7 Mix together all the punch ingredients except the orange slices in a large pitcher and stir until well blended. Refrigerate for at least 4 hours or up to overnight to allow the flavors to blend.

8 At party time, remove the punch bowl from the freezer and the pitcher from the refrigerator. Pour the punch into the bowl, garnish with the orange slices, and serve. You'll have hours of fun watching our party girl's demise!

YELLOW

snow cone

* * *

This lemony snowball has a frosty bite. Lemon ice is heaped into icy martini glasses, forming great big snowballs. Each guest drizzles their own snow cone with a little Limoncello liqueur. But be warned, this stuff is quite potent! This recipe can be made with real snow, but make sure it's clean! (As your parents may have told you, it's best to stay away from real yellow snow.)

Since most of the fun will come in the activity of drizzling yellow liquid over the snow, make sure to choose a cool container for the Limoncello syrup. An olive-oil dispenser works nicely. Keep an eye out for the guy who drizzles his name on his snow cone.

YOU WILL NEED

For the snow cone
One 12-ounce can frozen lemonade
   concentrate, thawed
3 cups ice
1 cup water
4 ounces Grand Marnier or Cointreau
⅓ cup sugar
8 martini glasses

For the Limoncello syrup
¼ cup sugar
¼ cup boiling water
¼ cup Limoncello
1 drop yellow food coloring
Candied lemon peel

Serves VIII

1 Process all the snow-cone ingredients in a food processor until the ice becomes slushy.

2 Pour into one of those plastic disposable 8-by-8-by-2-inch plastic pans (they are flexible and easy to use). Freeze for about 1 hour.

3 Scoop back into the food processor and blend until velvety smooth.

4 Freeze overnight, stirring once an hour for the first 3 hours.

✳ ✳ ✳

5 Scoop the snow into martini glasses and freeze for a few hours before serving.

6 Meanwhile, to make the syrup, in a bowl, combine the sugar and boiling water and stir until the sugar is dissolved. Stir in the Limoncello and food coloring. Transfer to a decorative decanter and cool. Pass the Limoncello syrup for dosing to taste.

7 Garnish with the candied lemon peel.

Real-Snow Yellow Snow Cone

For a real-snow version of the Yellow Snow Cone, first mix the lemonade concentrate, Cointreau, and sugar with a spoon in the 8-by-8-by-2-inch container. Set in the freezer for 45 minutes, then stir in 4 cups of fresh, clean snow. Place in the freezer, stirring every now and then to keep the mixture from freezing solid. When the consistency seems right, scoop into martini glasses and place in freezer until ready to serve with the Limoncello syrup.

KITSCHMAS

jigglepolitan

✳ ✳ ✳

"And he shook when he laughed like a bowlful of Jell-O!" Here's a swanky twist on frat-party favorite Jell-O shots. The nostalgic kitsch factor of gelatin desserts combines with the popularity of Cosmopolitans to give a kick you haven't felt since you got lost looking for your dorm room.

YOU WILL NEED

One 3-ounce box sparkling white
   grape–flavored gelatin
¾ cup boiling water
½ ounce Rose's Lime Juice
1½ ounces vodka
1 ounce Cointreau
3 ounces cranberry juice
2 small metal tart molds
2 martini glasses
1 toothpick (optional)

Serves II

NOTE
Choose fancy martini glasses that really accentuate the Jell-O experience. The glass shown here is ribbed and looks like a gelatin dessert already. There are many styles of glass out there that will also complement this wiggling, jiggling cocktail.

1 In a bowl, mix the gelatin with the boiling water and stir until dissolved, about 2 minutes. Refrigerate for 10 minutes.

2 Stir in the lime juice, vodka, Cointreau, and cranberry juice. Gently pour into the metal tart molds, filling them to the brim.

3 Pour the rest into the martini glasses. Pop all surface bubbles with the toothpick. Place in the refrigerator for at least 4 hours.

4 When the gelatin is firm, remove the glasses and tart molds from the refrigerator.

5 Dip a small, thin-bladed knife in warm water and run the tip of it around the edge of the molds to loosen.

6 Dip one mold in warm (not hot) water just barely below the rim for 10 seconds. Still holding the mold upright, shake the mold ever so slightly to loosen it from the sides. If we were unmolding a big Jell-O salad, we would place a chilled wet plate on top and flip it. That is not going to work with this recipe. You are going to have to be brave, be careful, and a little luck wouldn't hurt. Aim for the center of the waiting martini glass and hope for the best. (If the molded gelatin doesn't land dead center, who cares? Everyone is going to be slurping down a bunch of alcohol in a minute and no one will remember a thing.) Repeat with remaining mold and martini glass and serve.

RUDOLPH
the rehab reindeer's nose

* * *

So that's why his nose is so red! It isn't easy being the most famous reindeer of all! The highs, the lows, the intense pressure. Like many celebrities, Rudolph has taken twelve steps forward and twelve steps back, again and again. He has danced the Rehabilitation Rhumba many times over. Salute his struggle with this rosy treat.

YOU WILL NEED

Powdered sugar for rimming the glass
1 Champagne flute
3 ounces sparkling wine (don't use real Champagne; it's already perfect)
1 ounce Cointreau
1 ounce orange-flavored vodka
Pinch of granulated sugar
1 maraschino cherry for garnish

Serves 1

1 Place some powdered sugar on a plate. Moisten the rim of the glass and dip into the sugar.

2 Combine the sparkling wine, Cointreau, vodka, and granulated sugar in the Champagne flute. Drop in the cherry nose.

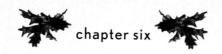

chapter six

Don We Now
Our Gay Apparel!

It seems that holiday fashions have pretty much followed the history of the holiday tree. As the trees got more gaudy, so did the clothing. From Victorian times, when festive hats and furs were dusted off to celebrate the season, to today's once-a-year, elfin outfits, we seem to be competing with the living-room evergreen for the Kitschmas spotlight.

Face it, holiday-themed clothing is, by definition, a fashion faux pas. You don't see supermodels working the runway in their reindeer sweaters. But Kitschmas isn't the season to shoot for chic. So go ahead: stroll your local suburban shopping mall (a.k.a. the Kitschmas Katwalk) and witness the procession of bejeweled vests and puffy paint sweatshirts. Accept it, embrace it, and surrender to the glitter god.

Now that you're emotionally prepared to don your gay apparel, the question is, How can you really stand out in a sea of sequins? The following pages take on this challenge by pushing holiday haute couture to the hilt, with little or no regard for restraint or aesthetic decency.

Strut your stuff baby, it's Kitschmas! Don you now your Protective Plastic Eating Poncho (left, page 109), or the Why Do You Think They Call it a Tree Skirt? (right, page 108).

WHY DO YOU THINK
they call it a tree skirt?

✳ ✳ ✳

Can't find anything to wear? Look under the tree! Not inside a brightly wrapped present—look under the gifts! Try that tree skirt on for size! There's no reason the tree should look better than you. Great-looking vintage tree skirts can be easily found at swap meets and online auction sites. They are usually so ornate that little needs to be done to make them more merry. Just a few alterations, a zipper, some trim, and a bold black belt and you'll go down in history!

YOU WILL NEED

1 dazzling tree skirt
A complete sewing kit
1 zipper
1 broad belt with a big brass buckle
About 20 jingle bells

1 Since tree skirts, like people, come in many different sizes, this project will take a little creativity, flexibility, and ingenuity on your part, not to mention sewing skills. Start by finding a tree skirt that suits your fancy and your girth. (Search online auction sites and swap meets if the one in your attic doesn't fit the bill.)

2 Devise an alteration plan, using a favorite skirt that fits you well as a pattern. Since very few people have a waist the size of a Scotch pine trunk, you will need to cut a larger waist. One easy way to solve this problem is to consider the possibility of layering it over an existing skirt, creating an apronlike festive flounce.

3 Cut and hem to a flattering length, and add a zipper (according to your plan of attack).

4 Hide any less-than-perfect sewing around the waist with the broad Santa-like belt.

5 As a nice finishing touch, sew a number of bells along the hemline to add a little jingle to your jiggle this holiday season.

PROTECTIVE PLASTIC
eating poncho

✳ ✳ ✳

This project is the perfect festive example of form following function. If your holidays are all about the buffet table, this may be the look for you. Using an old holiday-print vinyl tablecloth, cut a hole in the center. Finish the raw edges to soften the neckline and you're ready to chow down. It's simple, it's easy, it's vinyl for easy cleanups, and it hides a multitude of figure flaws so you can return to the food table as many times as you like with confidence.

YOU WILL NEED

One 60-inch round holiday-themed, vinyl-coated tablecloth
Iron
Scissors
Straight pins
6 yards of ¾-inch red pom-pom trim
Sewing machine or needle and thread
Sixteen 4-inch synthetic poinsettias

1 Start by pressing the table cloth with a cool iron, not hot, or it will all end in a big sticky mess.

2 Fold the tablecloth in half. Press along folded side with cool iron. Fold it again so that it's now in quarters. Press along new fold with the cool iron.

3 With scissors, cut off the pointy end to create a hole large enough to fit your head through.

4 Pin the pom-pom trim to the edge of the tablecloth and sew together with the sewing machine, or by hand if you must.

5 Sew the poinsettias around the collar to soften the neckline and hide the unfinished edge.

6 Slip the poncho over your head, it's time to eat!

MERRY JANES

* * *

Okay, so *The Wizard of Oz* is not a Christmas story, per se. Still, it's shown every year during the holidays, perhaps because that's when there's no place like home. Isn't that what this season is all about? Oh yes, and a key plot point takes shape in the form of a big nasty catfight over a pair of fabulous pumps. Reminiscent of holiday shoe sales, perhaps? Resurrect your old bridesmaid pumps (that you swore you'd be able to wear again) for these glittering beauties, guaranteed to put some twinkle on your toes.

YOU WILL NEED

1 pair of satin pumps
One 1-inch flat craft brush
One 8-ounce bottle of liquid red fabric dye (standard issue such as Rit—no fancy shoe dye required)
A wad of beeswax
One 8-inch or smaller bamboo skewer
About 1,000 red 10-mm sequins
Hot-glue gun and glue sticks
About 1,000 red 7-mm acrylic faceted gemstones
Strong needle and red thread
Two 4-inch lengths of ½-inch white elastic
About 30 red seed beads
2 small artificial holly decorations to fancy up the straps

1   This project starts in the dark recesses of your closet. There you will find a collection of bridesmaid shoes, in colors with names like peach, sea foam, lilac, and blush. Choose the color most likely to make a nice shade of red. Using the craft brush, paint the shoes with the liquid dye as quickly and as evenly as possible. Let the shoes dry completely.

2   Make a great gem pick-up tool by forming a cotton-swab-shaped beeswax tip on the blunt end of the bamboo skewer. You will use the beeswax end to pick up the sequins and gemstones and the pointed end to position them. You won't believe how great this little tool works.

3   Using your groovy new tool, pick up a sequin, concave-side down. Apply a dab of hot glue (starting at the back of the shoe) and place the sequin over the glue. It will practically melt into place. Repeat, trying to keep the sequins as close together as possible, until both shoes are completely covered.

4   Now, hot-glue a gemstone to the center of each sequin on the shoes.

5 With red thread, sew sequins to the elastic straps using a red seed bead on each sequin to ensure a secure placement and a little extra zing. Finish them off with the fancy holly atop each strap.

6 Click your cha-cha heels together three times and sing, "There's No Place Like Home for the Holidays!"

FASHION STATEMENT
sweatshirts

✳ ✳ ✳

The phenomenon of homemade holiday sweatshirts is a recent craft craze that is building a better tomorrow for future kitsch collectors. There is very little anyone could do to kitsch it up a notch, as people seem to be doing quite nicely on their own. In fact, these courageous artists deserve praise and applause for their gumption, nerve, and commitment to spreading the Kitschmas spirit. Still, there is always room for improvement and impertinence.

Let's be honest: no matter how festive or merry, these things make us look like elves stuffed in a decorated felt stocking. So, since honesty is the best policy, and these fashion statements say so much about the person who wears them, may we suggest the use of words to articulate that fashion statement more clearly. Go out and get yourself a huge red sweatshirt, sheets of felt in assorted colors, sequins, seed beads, puff paint, and pom-pom trim, and get ready to tell the truth about the sweatshirts and those of us who have the guts to wear them.

Try the following fashion-statement ideas for size:

- You think this is gaudy, you should see my tree!

- I have an OCD

- I ♥ glitter

- Someone made this for me and I feel obligated to wear it

- When bad holiday fashions happen to good people

- I look like a parade float (opposite)

KITSCHMAS
koiffures!

✳ ✳ ✳

One woman's hairdo is definitely another's hair-don't, but if you're looking to go all out this Kitschmas (hey, you've already gotten this far), you might consider the traffic-stopping possibilities of a festive coif. Obviously, these 'dos are most appropriate for parties, but you can always set the office on its ear by just showing up at your desk and acting as if nothing is out of the ordinary.

The use of wigs is strongly suggested here, for many reasons: **A)** Very few people have enough hair to successfully achieve these fabulous results. **B)** You might end up buying a wig anyway after torturing your hair into shape and it falls out. This could end in tears! And **C)** If you get called into the human resources office to get written up for distracting attire, you can always remove it, plead innocent, and finish your workday.

OPPOSITE **Let It FRO, Let It FRO, Let It FRO**

The secret to this wig is density, not size. This seemingly easy project can go terribly wrong if you do not use restraint. You can easily get caught up in making this the biggest Afro ever, but before you do, stop: put down the pick, back away from the wig, and take a deep, cleansing breath. The idea is to make a rigid, round, snowball-like shape. This is best achieved with tons of hair spray, careful sculpting, and spray glitter.

✳ ✳ ✳

OPPOSITE **Hark! The Farrah Angel Wings!**

Back in the seventies, this hairstyle swept through the halls of high schools everywhere like a contagious virus. Each girl had her own take on "the Farrah" look. Some attempts were more successful than others. If you couldn't tousle your hair into this shape, you sprayed the hell out of it or used a curling iron to burn it into a series of flippy little flaps of hair. These "flaps" were commonly referred to as "wings." By no means was this a coincidence: Farrah was heavenly in her mane of gold and the most memorable of all the Angels. You too can look angelic with this hairstyle, along with a white polyester stretch jumpsuit for ease of movement in the event of a kung fu confrontation with a bad guy.

PAGE 118 **That Kissmas Girl!**

If you are old enough to remember Marlo Thomas's trademark flip in the sixties television series *That Girl,* you know that this look is all about a spunky single girl in the city with a purseful of dreams. If this describes your situation-comedy life and the wig fits, wear it. The mod headband is embellished with plastic mistletoe so you're always in the right place at the right time for love.

PAGE 2 **Kitschmas Tree Hive**

This grand-finale hair project is by far the most challenging. It might be best left to seasoned professionals. The skills needed to achieve this hairstravaganza are hard earned and take years of practice. Here are three suggestions on how to get this look.

1 Go to a local wig/costume shop and show them this photo.

2 Drive to the outskirts of town, find a truck stop or trailer park, then search out the closest beauty shoppe. Look for the telltale spelling of the word "shoppe."

3 Oh, just find a drag queen and ask her to work her magic.

Table of Equivalents

The exact equivalents in the following tables have been rounded for convenience.

Liquid/Dry Measures

U.S.	Metric
¼ teaspoon	1.25 milliliters
½ teaspoon	2.5 milliliters
1 teaspoon	5 milliliters
1 tablespoon (3 teaspoons)	15 milliliters
1 fluid ounce (2 tablespoons)	30 milliliters
¼ cup	60 milliliters
⅓ cup	80 milliliters
½ cup	120 milliliters
1 cup	240 milliliters
1 pint (2 cups)	480 milliliters
1 quart (4 cups; 32 ounces)	960 milliliters
1 gallon (4 quarts)	3.84 liters
1 ounce (by weight)	28 grams
1 pound	454 grams
2.2 pounds	1 kilogram

Length

U.S.	Metric
⅛ inch	3 millimeters
¼ inch	6 millimeters
½ inch	12 millimeters
1 inch	2.5 centimeters

Oven Temperature

Fahrenheit	Celsius	Gas
250	120	½
275	140	1
300	150	2
325	160	3
350	180	4
375	190	5
400	200	6
425	220	7
450	230	8
475	240	9
500	260	10

Merry Kitschmas to all
and to all a good night!

The wreaths and the stockings are all hung with care,
On top of your head is a tree made of hair.

With you and the twinkle lights, both brightly lit,
You loosen your belt and finally sit.

You cooked like a fiend, you're full as a tick,
You ate figgy pudding until you were sick.

For weeks you have sequined, and sculpted, and painted,
You hot-glued your fingers 'til nearly you fainted.

Why? you may ask yourself, Why all this panic,
When all of it ends up just boxed in the attic?

And just when you think you're too old for all this,
You hear a reminder of why you love kitsch.

Oh no! Andy Williams! It's his voice you hear,
This IS the most wonderful time of the year!